THE ANGEL
BY GAVIN BIGGS
ILLUSTRATED BY AGILULFO RUSSO

ABOUT YOUR BOOK

	Listen to the story and activities on the HELBLING Media App
Listen in	Develop active listening skills on the HELBLING Media App
	Talk about the story
glossary•	When you see the red dot, check the word in the glossary
K	Prepare for Cambridge English Exams: A2 Key
e•	Go to ezone.helbling.com to do the activities

FOR THE TEACHER

e• Go to HELBLING e-zone for Cyber Homework, downloadable worksheets, answer keys and Reading Matters, the Teacher's Guide to using Helbling Readers in your class.

For a full list of both classic and fiction titles go to helbling.com/english

Contents

HELBLING DIGITAL

INTERACTIVE ONLINE TEACHING AND LEARNING MATERIALS

e·ZONE
THE EDUCATIONAL PLATFORM

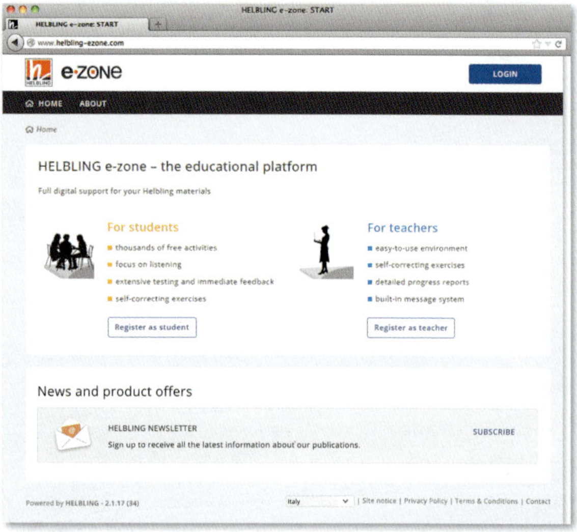

HELBLING e-zone is an inspiring new state-of-the-art, easy-to-use interactive learning environment.

Use the **personal access code** on the inside front cover of this book to unlock a host of self-correcting activities, including:

- reading comprehension;
- listening comprehension;
- vocabulary;
- grammar;
- exam preparation.

TEACHERS register free of charge to set up classes and assign individual and class homework sets. Results are provided automatically once the deadline has been reached and detailed reports on performance are available at a click.

STUDENTS test their language skills in a stimulating interactive environment. All activities can be attempted as many times as necessary and full results and feedback are given as soon as the deadline has been reached. Single student access is also available.

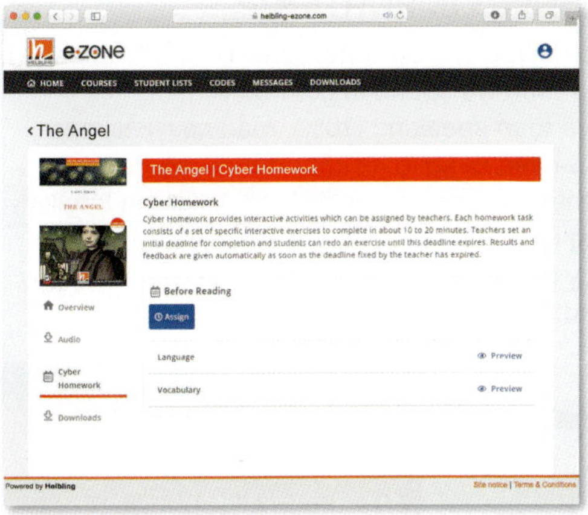

1000s of free online interactive activities now available for HELBLING READERS and your other favourite Helbling Languages publications.

ONLINE ACTIVITIES

ezone.helbling.com

helbling.com/readersblog

Love reading and readers and can't wait to get your class interested? Have a class library and reading programme but not sure how to take it a step further? The Helbling Readers BLOG is the place for you.

The **Helbling Readers BLOG** will provide you with ideas on setting up and running a Book Club and tips on reading lessons **every week**.

- Book Club
- Worksheets
- Lesson Plans

Subscribe to our **BLOG** and you will never miss out on our updates.

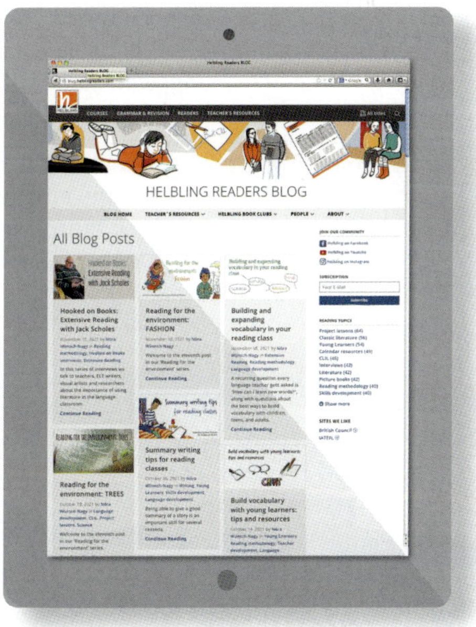

Listen in

Listen in is a new series of readers with a special focus on developing your students' active listening skills.

WHY IS LISTENING IMPORTANT?

Listening is key to **effective communication**. It occupies about 45% of the time we spend in communication. Significantly more than speaking (30%), reading (16%) and writing (9%)[1]. However, despite its importance, students say that listening is the most challenging of the 4 skills in English. The new Helbling Readers series, ***Listen in***, aims to redress this imbalance by developing your students' active listening skills as they read.

Over 60% of all misunderstandings come from poor listening, only 1% from poor reading[2].

WHAT IS ACTIVE LISTENING?

Listening and **reading** are often defined as **receptive skills**, because learners do not need to produce language to do them. While speaking and writing are known as productive skills. All skills are integrated and support each other in the process of learning, with students typically beginning with a receptive understanding of new language before developing a productive one.

Active listening is paying attention to a spoken text in order to fully understand the meaning of the words and the intentions of the speaker. Active listening helps students not only in their **learning**, but also in their **self-esteem** and **self-efficacy**. It teaches students to **communicate** their ideas and also to **think critically**. Plus, active listening promotes **mindfulness** and **empathy**.

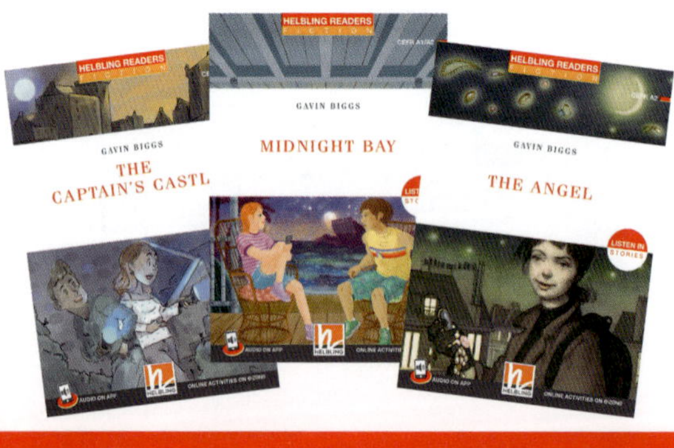

In the ***Listen in*** series, readers help the main characters to solve an exciting mystery by listening in to vital information and collecting clues. Active listening skills are developed through a variety of Before, While and After Reading activities.

Just look out for the **Listen in** box.

PRE-TEACHING KEY VOCABULARY

PRICELESS SWORD STOLEN!

1 Listen to this news report about another theft from the Louvre Museum in 1976. Then answer the questions.

a What type of sword is it?

1 ☐ emerald 2 ☐ garnet 3 ☐ diamond

b In which year was the sword made?

1 ☐ 1824 2 ☐ 1924 3 ☐ 1976

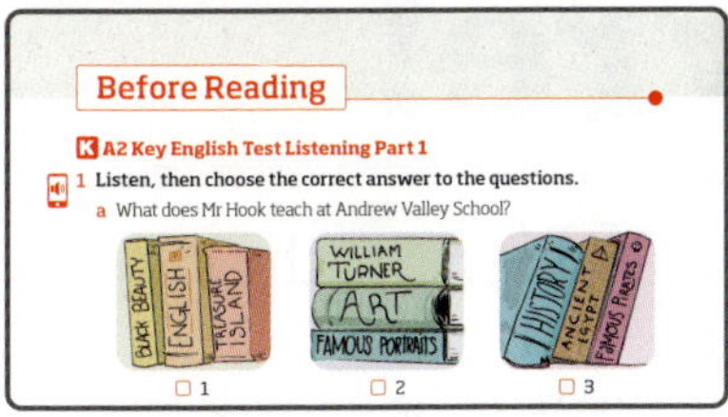
Before Reading

A2 Key English Test Listening Part 1

1 Listen, then choose the correct answer to the questions.

a What does Mr Hook teach at Andrew Valley School?

☐ 1 ☐ 2 ☐ 3

ACTIVATING BACKGROUND KNOWLEDGE

Special **Listen in** pages after each chapter develop active listening strategies and work on the following listening skills:

- Listening to distinguish words and expressions (discriminative listening);
- Listening for details and information (precise listening);
- Listening for general understanding (listening for gist and summarising);
- Evaluating and analysing (listening for inference).

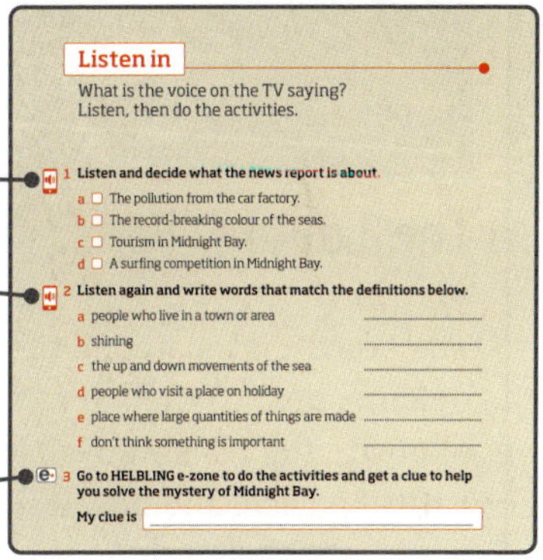
Listen in

What is the voice on the TV saying? Listen, then do the activities.

1 Listen and decide what the news report is about.

a ☐ The pollution from the car factory.
b ☐ The record-breaking colour of the seas.
c ☐ Tourism in Midnight Bay.
d ☐ A surfing competition in Midnight Bay.

2 Listen again and write words that match the definitions below.

a people who live in a town or area ....
b shining ....
c the up and down movements of the sea ....
d people who visit a place on holiday ....
e place where large quantities of things are made ....
f don't think something is important ....

3 Go to HELBLING e-zone to do the activities and get a clue to help you solve the mystery of Midnight Bay.

My clue is ....

DEBATE

After Reading

Listen in and Debate

Can young people make a real difference to the environment?

1 We asked this question to four teenagers. Who agrees? Listen and tick (✓).

2 Listen again and write the correct names.

3 Think. Who do you agree with?

WHAT ARE FOSSIL FUELS?

4 What are fossil fuels used for? Tick (✓) below, then share ideas with a friend. Listen and check.

What are the problems with fossil fuels?

5 Read, then complete the text with the missing words.

6 In two groups, discuss the question below. Do you agree? Say why, or why not. Give reasons and examples. Use the quotes to help.

Can young people make a real difference to the environment?

I AGREE GRETA THUNBERG (Activist)

I DISAGREE ARNOLD SCHWARZENEGGER (Actor and politician)

LISTENING AND SPEAKING

Listen in and Speak and **Listen in and Debate** spreads take learners from attentive listening to critical response and help develop all-important **oracy skills**.

PRONUNCIATION PRACTICE

Throughout each book special ***Listen in*** boxes focus on **pronunciation**.

Listen in

4 Listen and repeat the words with *p* and *b*.

pirate - mo**b**ile climb - cam**p**
patch - **b**ag **p**ush - **b**ush
place - **b**lack **p**ort - **b**oth

NOTES

[1] Raphael Ahmed for *The British Council*.

[2] Iwankovitsch, R. *The Importance of Listening*.

STOLEN FROM THE Louvre!

The Louvre, Paris.

The Louvre is located in the centre of Paris, next to the river Seine, and opposite the Palais-Royal. It was once a royal palace, and now it's the world's most popular museum. It is home to some of the most famous paintings in the world. Its biggest attraction• is *The Mona Lisa*, by the Italian artist, Leonardo da Vinci. Over 80% of the people who visit the museum, go there to see this painting, which even has its own post box, because it receives so many love letters!
The museum also has an impressive• collection of sculptures•, including two masterpieces• from Ancient Greece, *Venus de Milo* and the *Winged Victory of Samothrace*. One of these sculptures is important in this story. Look through the illustrations and find which one.

A thief• in the night

The Mona Lisa wasn't especially• famous before it was stolen in 1911. The theft• was in all the newspapers, and it shocked the world. The thief was an Italian artist Vincenzo Peruggia, who wanted to return the painting to its home country.
Vincenzo hid in a cupboard during the night, then left the museum with the *Mona Lisa*, without anyone seeing him. In fact, no one noticed the painting was missing for 24 hours. He hid the painting for two years, but he was arrested• when he tried to sell it in 1913. It is now safely back at the Louvre.

- **arrested:** taken to a police station to be questioned about a crime
- **attraction:** thing people want to see
- **especially:** more than usual
- **impressive:** amazing; very important
- **masterpieces:** very important works
- **priceless:** very expensive
- **sculptures:** statues
- **theft:** the act of stealing
- **thief:** someone who steals

OVER TO YOU

Find out more about the *Venus de Milo* or the *Winged Victory of Samothrace*. Share your findings in class.

PRICELESS SWORD STOLEN!

1 Listen to this news report about another theft from the Louvre Museum in 1976. Then answer the questions.

a What type of sword is it?

1 ☐ emerald 2 ☐ garnet 3 ☐ diamond

b In which year was the sword made?

1 ☐ 1824 2 ☐ 1924 3 ☐ 1976

c What did the thieves break?

1 ☐ the window
2 ☐ the glass case
3 ☐ the king's sword

d This is a real news story. Find out online where the sword is now.

Listen in

2 Listen and repeat the sentence. Pay attention to the underlined parts of the words.

Three thieves climbed through a window.

3 Listen to these words. Repeat the words with a partner to practise the difference.

thick / tick	three / tree	both / boat
theme / team	thief / teeth	path / part

4 Listen and tick (✓) the words you hear.

a That ☐ part / ☐ path by the river is my favourite place in Paris.
b He looked closely at the ☐ thief / ☐ teeth.
c Can you bring those ☐ three / ☐ tree books to my study?

THE ANGEL

1 **Listen and decide who is speaking. Write the letters beside the pictures.**

2 **Look at the pictures and find someone:**

- **a** who has a moustache,
- **b** who is wearing large vintage glasses,
- **c** who is wearing a red suit,
- **d** who is bald,
- **e** who looks younger than everyone else.

3 **Share your answers to Exercise 2 with a friend.**

Before Reading

1 Match the words to the things in the collection room. Use a dictionary if necessary.

- ▢ bracelet
- ▢ brooch
- ▢ column
- ▢ crown
- ▢ diamond
- ▢ earring
- ▢ necklace
- ▢ painting
- ▢ ring
- ▢ ruby
- ▢ statue
- ▢ glass cases

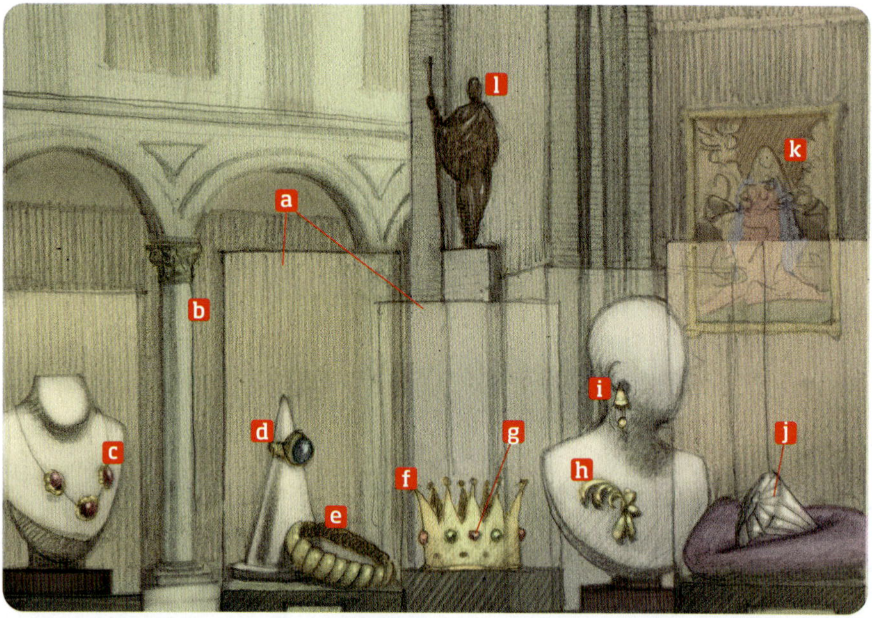

2 Use the words from Exercise 1 to complete the sentences.

a The collection room was full of ...., each one with a piece of jewellery inside.

b She held up the pair of ruby .... to the light. They were beautiful.

c In the Louvre, there is a .... of the goddess *Nike*. It looked like an angel.

d Angelica climbed up a .... and ran along the top wall of the palace.

e All the jewels were stolen from Louis XV's ...., including the famous Regent diamond .

Listen in

3 Listen to the pronunciation of the word *ruby* in these sentences. Then repeat the sentences with a partner.

A *ruby* is a dark red stone or jewel.
She stole Empress Josephine's *ruby* necklace.

4 Listen and tick (✓) the words that have the same sound as the vowel in ruby.

- ☐ clue
- ☐ food
- ☐ jewel
- ☐ music
- ☐ could
- ☐ good
- ☐ moved
- ☐ put

5 Look at the pictures of rooms from *The Angel*. Then match them with the descriptions below.

a collection room

b conference room

c hall

d living room

e reception room

f study

1 ☐ This room is used for events and parties.
2 ☐ This is used for working or studying.
3 ☐ A space to display items of value, such as jewellery or paintings.
4 ☐ This room is inside a home and is used for relaxing.
5 ☐ This room is used for meetings.
6 ☐ This is a long passage that leads to other rooms.

Before Reading

K A2 Key English Test Listening Part 1

1 Listen, then choose the correct answer to the questions.

a What do Angelica's family think she does for a job?

☐ 1

☐ 2

☐ 3

b Which sport did Porter do when he was younger?

☐ 1

☐ 2

☐ 3

c What did Teddy study?

☐ 1

☐ 2

☐ 3

d What is Madame Helene's favourite project?

☐ 1

☐ 2

☐ 3

K A2 Key English Test Listening Part 3

2 Read the questions. Listen to Detective Champion and Sergeant Gabriel, then choose the correct answers.

a Where are they?
1 ☐ outside the Palais-Royal
2 ☐ in a police car
3 ☐ at the police station

b How far away from the Palais-Royal are they?
1 ☐ 10 minutes
2 ☐ 23 minutes
3 ☐ 25 minutes

c How long has Detective Champion been a detective?
1 ☐ 20 years
2 ☐ 25 years
3 ☐ more than 25 years

d Who turns on the police sirens?
1 ☐ Detective Champion
2 ☐ Sergeant Gabriel
3 ☐ the Angel

e Who thinks the Angel is a great problem to solve?
1 ☐ Detective Champion
2 ☐ Detective Champion's father
3 ☐ Sergeant Gabriel

3 Listen to Detective Champion. Take notes, then in pairs see how much you remember.

Before Reading

Think and Predict

1 Read an extract from the beginning of the book. Then answer the questions.

A figure in a long grey coat climbed out of a window, and ran silently into the shadows of the many columns of the Palais-Royal. It was a dark, wet evening in Paris. A cold fog from the river Seine was beginning to cover the streets. The streetlights made moving shadows in the fog. It was a perfect evening to steal Empress Josephine's ruby necklace. And one or two other things.

Angelica pulled her coat closer to her neck and tightened the straps on her backpack. She could feel the extra weight of the necklace inside it.

a Who is the figure in the long grey coat?
b What is in the backpack?
c Why is it a 'perfect evening' to steal something?

2 Guess. What happens next in the story? Share your ideas with a partner.

3 Look at the pictures. Then discuss the questions with a partner. What do you think?

a What is the meaning of the feather?
b Who does the crown belong to?
c Where is the statue?

4 Think about the statement below. Do you agree with it? Why / Why not? Discuss ideas with a friend.

It is always wrong to steal things.

1 Angelica

A figure in a long grey coat climbed out of a window, and ran silently into the shadows• of the many columns of the Palais-Royal. It was a dark, wet evening in Paris. A cold fog from the river Seine was beginning to cover the streets. The streetlights made moving shadows in the fog. It was a perfect evening to steal Empress Josephine's ruby necklace. And one or two other things.

Angelica pulled her coat closer to her neck and tightened• the straps on her backpack. She could feel the extra weight of the necklace inside it. She checked her watch – it was too early to leave.

She walked casually• in the shadows. She was good at it. People didn't notice• her. But this evening she could feel something. Was someone watching her? She decided to get a better viewpoint.

In a few seconds, she climbed a column and ran along the top wall. She jumped across a gap• between the buildings, threw a rope over a statue on the roof, and climbed up. She sat next to the statue, and looked down at the courtyard• of the Palais-Royal and the gardens beyond it.

GLOSSARY

- **casually:** in a relaxed way
- **courtyard:** large area in front of a palace or big house
- **gap:** empty space
- **notice:** see
- **shadows:** dark areas where the light does not fall
- **tightened:** (here) made shorter

Was there someone in the gardens? She thought she saw something move. She looked down – she could hear sirens•. The police were finally here! She checked her watch. It had taken them 15 minutes! Far too slow, as usual. She watched the blue flashing lights go down the road and through the gates.

She sat on the top of the Palais-Royal with her legs over the edge•. She was bored. Another brilliant theft of priceless• jewellery. Ten years of planning and carrying out• the most difficult and dangerous thefts, but it wasn't the same anymore.

The police were running into the old palace now. She could hear them talking to the guards. A bigger car arrived, and two men stepped out. One was tall and had a moustache. Angelica smiled. She knew him well. Detective Champion – head of the Major Crimes Unit•. *How many years is it now?* she asked herself. *He'll never give up•* – *but he'll never catch• me!*

GLOSSARY

- **carrying out:** doing
- **catch:** find and stop (a criminal)
- **edge:** (here) highest point
- **give up:** stop doing something
- **major crimes unit:** part of the police that solves important cases
- **priceless:** very expensive
- **sirens:** sound on police cars, etc

She didn't know the second man. He was younger, tall and slim, with short, dark hair. He wasn't talking to the guards. He was looking up at the buildings. She stopped moving. Was he looking directly at her? Could he really see her on the roof?

'THE ANGEL?!' she heard a voice shout. 'NOOOO!'

It was the detective. He was angry. Very angry. A guard was holding a white feather in his hand. Angelica's feather, her angel wings. Her name was Angelica, but everyone knew her as 'the Angel'. The best thief in the world.

The detective had reason• to be angry – twenty years of chasing• the Angel. But he didn't know that Angelica was the *second* Angel. The first Angel stopped working ten years ago. She was his apprentice•. Angelica thought back. There were three of them then – the Angel, the Phoenix and Angelica. The Phoenix's real name was Terence. He was the same age as Angelica, and together they learned all the skills to become the best thieves in the world. But after a final test, the Angel chose Angelica. Then he retired•, went to live on an island, and she became the new Angel. Terence lost. He was so angry that he left Paris. Of course, the detective didn't know these things. He thought that he was still chasing the same person.

Poor Detective Champion. But it was time for a new Angel soon. Angelica watched him as he spoke to a police officer, then she ran along the walls and down the side of the building into the gardens. She was like a ghost. She ran down to the river. A small motorboat was coming. A big man with a blue hat was behind the wheel. The boat slowed down as it came past Angelica to let her jump on board•.

'Good evening, Porter,' she said to the man.

'Good evening, Miss,' he said. 'Home?'

'Yes Porter, take me home, please,' she said.

- **apprentice:** person who learns how to do something from another person
- **chasing:** going after; following
- **had reason:** was right
- **on board:** onto (a boat or plane, etc)
- **retired:** stopped working

Listen in

What does Detective Champion say to the police officer? Listen, then do the activities.

1 Listen and tick (✓) the word in each pair that you hear.

a ☐ clever	☐ feather	**c** ☐ door	☐ tore	**e** ☐ nice	☐ noise
b ☐ clue	☐ glue	**d** ☐ cards	☐ guards	**f** ☐ set	☐ sit

2 Listen again, complete the officer's notes.

Guards were about ....
door, when they .... a noise.
They went to .... - think
that .... came in then.

3 Go to HELBLING e-zone to do the activities and get a clue to help you solve the mystery of the Angel.

My clue is ....

2 Porter

Angelica sat in her study with the contents of her backpack on her desk. The study was large and luxurious. There were soft armchairs and beautiful painted walls, bronze statues, and a row• of bookcases. A fire burned in the wide fireplace. Paintings of famous French women covered the walls.

She looked at the necklace in front of her. It was very beautiful. She took the other item• and held it up to the light. Gold and jewels. Her life was gold and jewels. She pressed a secret button under her desk, and a bookcase in the wall opened like a door. She took the jewellery and went into her collection• room. The room was very big, and it was full of glass cases, one hundred to be precise. Inside each one there was a light and a card with a description of the jewellery. Only two of the cases were empty. She opened these cases now and put the two new stolen items inside. Then she took a deep breath, and looked around. Her collection was complete. Ten years! Ten years and one hundred pieces of the most famous jewellery in the world. That was the promise• she made to the first Angel, all those years ago.

GLOSSARY

- **collection:** group of the same type of item
- **item:** thing
- **promise:** something you say that you will certainly do
- **row:** line

She walked up and down the rows of glass cases, reliving• the memories she had for each piece of jewellery. *All that planning,* she thought. *And without anyone knowing how I did it or who I am.* She turned around and went back to her study, closing the bookcase door behind her.

There was a laptop on the desk in front of her. Her secret email account was open – but there were no messages. She hoped to find a new Angel, a replacement•, but it was difficult. She wanted to retire, but only when she found the right person. She read every news story of every theft in every country, but no one seemed right. She looked on secret websites where thieves came to sell their stolen items. She left clues and puzzles, but no one contacted her. Were her puzzles too difficult? No, she needed someone clever. Very clever. Her latest clue was now posted on every secret message board she knew.

GLOSSARY

• **reliving:** thinking about again

• **replacement:** (here) new Angel

'The path to Victory• is in the wings. The Sport of Art sees the way.' It was easy. Well, she thought it was... the 'Sport of Art' meant a statue in the Louvre, the statue of 'Winged Victory' of the goddess Nike. It was Porter's favourite statue, and sometimes they went to see it together. The statue looked like an angel, maybe that was why Porter liked it so much. Her email address was hidden on the wings of the statue.

Maybe it *was* a little difficult. Oh well. Angelica was hungry. She left her study and went into the kitchen. Porter was cooking. He looked happy – he loved cooking.

She watched him for a moment. He was her bodyguard, her assistant•, her chef and her only friend, really. He worked for the original Angel before Angelica. A famous boxer when he was young, he was now fat and bald•, and had hair in his ears, but he was still strong and loyal•. Something happened many years ago – the first Angel saved his life, although Angelica never knew how. He made a promise at that time to protect the Angel and then to protect Angelica, too.

Porter looked up.

'Dinner's nearly ready, Miss,' he said. 'I'll bring it into the dining room.'

'Thank you, Porter, but I think I'll eat in the living room tonight,' she said, taking a bottle of water from the fridge. Her house was large and bright•, with light wooden floors and high ceilings. There was even a garden, which was unusual in central Paris.

She went up the grand• staircase and into a smaller, more comfortable living room with soft sofas and chairs around a fireplace. Above the fireplace was a huge television. It didn't look right in the room, but Angelica didn't care. She enjoyed movies• too much. And watching the news – especially when it was about her! She lay down on the sofa and turned the TV on.

- **assistant:** helper
- **bald:** without hair
- **bright:** with lots of light
- **grand:** (here) big and beautiful
- **loyal:** that always stays with and supports another person
- **movies:** films
- **victory:** act of winning

Listen in

What does Angelica hear on the news? Listen, then do the activities.

1 Listen and tick (✓) what was stolen.

a ☐ They don't know.
b ☐ Cardinal Richelieu's post
c ☐ Empress Josephine's necklace
d ☐ A painting from the art collection

2 Listen again, take notes about the Palais-Royal.

Built:

Home to:

Famous for:

3 Go to HELBLING e-zone to do the activities and get a clue to help you solve the mystery of the Angel.

My clue is ....

3 Detective Champion

Men and women jumped to the side as the detective marched• down the hall. He was furious•. He was shouting one word over and over again.

Everyone in the police headquarters knew the detective. And they knew what happened when he said that word.

'Angel! ANGEL!' his voice became louder. 'ANGEL, ANGEL, ANGEL!'

He turned a corner and surprised a young officer. The officer jumped out of the way just in time. The detective didn't see him. He didn't see anyone. He marched and shouted and shouted and marched to his office.

He pushed open the door, and took a deep breath.

'I WANT ALL THE INFORMATION ON THE NECKLACE THEFT! AND I WANT IT–'

Before he could finish, a young man in an expensive suit walked up to him. He was tall and slim with short dark hair and he was holding a thick• report.

'You want it now, Sir?' said the man.

'YES! NOW!' he shouted. 'Thank you, Sergeant Gabriel!'

GLOSSARY

- **furious:** very angry
- **marched:** (here) walked quickly and noisily
- **thick:** (here) with lots of pages

'You're welcome, Sir,' said Sergeant Gabriel. 'Perhaps we can go into the conference room?'

'YES! We will go to the conference room! But first I want–'

'Your coffee? Here you are, Sir,' said Gabriel and put a small, but very strong cup of coffee in the detective's hand.

The detective didn't say anything. He took the coffee, drank it, and nodded at Gabriel. 'Good work,' he said and walked towards the conference room. Gabriel smiled and followed the detective.

Detective Champion was an excellent investigator. He was top of his class at the police academy. He *never* gave up. He looked at every clue. He spoke to every witness himself. He had an excellent memory. He spoke four languages, including Japanese. But, since the first Angel case twenty years ago, the detective could think of nothing but the Angel. It was the only case he couldn't solve. The most famous thief in the world – here in Paris!

GLOSSARY

- **conference:** large meeting
- **investigator:** police officer who solves crime cases
- **nodded:** moved his head to say 'yes'
- **perhaps:** maybe
- **top:** (here) best; number 1

Sergeant Gabriel was a little different. He was also top of his class at the academy, and he was an Olympic skiing champion. He was also fluent in many European languages. He was even a master of Chinese chess. He liked to solve problems. And that was the difference. Detective Champion was a traditional policeman. He wanted to stop bad things from happening. But Sergeant Gabriel saw everything as a problem to be solved. And now the Angel was his problem. And he was very, very happy.

'Why are you smiling, Gabriel?' asked the detective.

'This case, Sir!' he said, looking at the computer screens in the conference room, 'Look!'

He pointed at one of the screens. It was the room of the theft in the Palais-Royal. The detective couldn't see anything interesting on the screen.

'There's nothing there!' he said.

'Exactly! Now, look here...' Gabriel turned to another screen. It was a plan of the building. He turned to Detective Champion.

'I think that the only way to get to the necklace, without setting off• the alarm, is across the glass roof,' said Gabriel.

Detective Champion looked at the two screens.

'No, the Angel probably used ropes to get across the floor without touching it. Very clever!'

'Umm... no, Sir. There's nowhere to tie a rope. The Angel walked across the glass roof – and if the Angel walked across the glass roof, it means that he weighs 60 kg, or less. I think the Angel has to be a woman, Sir.'

The detective laughed. He laughed so loud everyone outside the office stopped working.

'That's impossible! Remember, I've seen the Angel! HE was tall and he looked strong. He was slim• yes, but also very tall and strong. I saw him... 12 years ago... I'll never forget...'

Gabriel sat down while the detective told his story. He knew the story already. Everyone knew the story already.

- **setting off:** (here) starting
- **slim:** thin

Listen in

What is Detective Champion's story? Listen, then do the activities.

1 Listen and tick (✓) what was stolen.

a ☐

b ☐
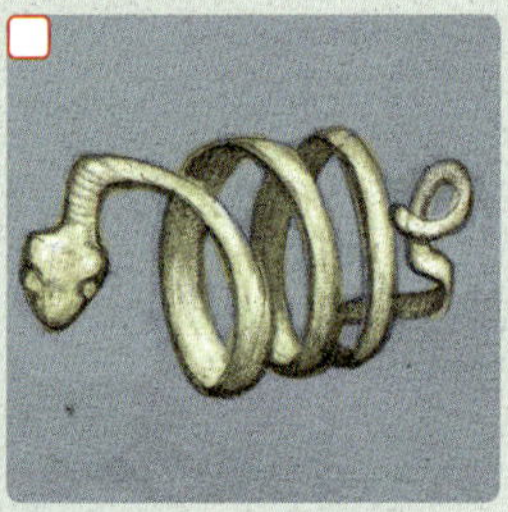

c ☐

2 Listen again and answer the questions.

a When is Bastille Day?

____

b Why was the Louvre so busy that day?

____

c Why were the thermal cameras not working in the Egyptian Room?

____

d Why did the police go to the Da Vinci room?

____

e Describe the man that Champion saw in the Egyptian room.

____

3 Go to HELBLING e-zone to do the activities and get a clue to help you solve the mystery of the Angel.

My clue is ....

4 Madame Helene

Gabriel turned on his laptop, and looked through all the files he had about the Angel. He wasn't sure how much to tell the detective. Perhaps just enough to make things difficult for the Angel? But Gabriel had his own plans, too.

'Sir? I have an idea.'

'Yes?'

'I'd like to introduce you to someone,' said Gabriel.

'A suspect?' asked Champion.

'No, the Head of Exhibitions at the Palais-Royal. She told me something very interesting, and I asked her to come here,' said Gabriel, opening the doors of the conference room.

'She wants a report on the necklace already?! It only happened last night!' Champion wasn't happy.

'No, Sir, it's about something else. I was thinking about the next item the Angel will steal, and there aren't that many famous pieces of jewellery left now. But there is one very famous crown. Ah! Here she is. She can tell you more,' said Gabriel.

A short woman in a white suit with large vintage• glasses came into the room. She was followed by a young man with spiky• hair and small eyes. He was wearing a red jacket and an orange shirt.

GLOSSARY

- **spiky:** that goes up in points
- **vintage:** classic (from the past)

Gabriel thought he looked like a chicken.
'Detective!' said the woman, 'I am Madame Helene.'
Detective Champion put on• his best smile.
'Welcome Madame! It is a pleasure• to meet you. I'd like to say how sorry I am about the theft of the necklace. We are looking for the thief.'
Madame Helene smiled. The detective was quite handsome.
'Thank you, Detective. And I am here to tell you something that may help *you* – Louis XV's crown!'
The detective looked at her.
'I'm sorry Madame, I don't understand. Has it been stolen?'
The man with the red jacket stepped forward and laughed.
'No, Detective. Louis XV's crown has been on display• in the Louvre for many years, but the stones in it are glass pieces, not the original ones.' Detective Champion coughed, he did not know this.
'Well,' the man continued, 'we have found all the original stones, including the famous Regent diamond. And tomorrow night it will go on display in the Palais-Royal where Louis XV lived.'
'Thank you, Teddy,' interrupted• Madame Helene. 'Teddy is my assistant,' she said, turning to the others. 'The event is top secret, of course. And only the most important people in Paris will be there. At the moment the crown and its jewels are safe in the Palais-Royal. But your sergeant, Gabriel, told me you have an idea...'
Detective Champion turned to look at his sergeant.
'Did he? And my idea, Sergeant?'
Sergeant Gabriel smiled.
'Your idea, Sir, is to catch the Angel with a trap•!'
'Aha! Well, a trap. The Angel will want to steal the crown. Uhmm... but in the same place? Only two days later?! It is very dangerous,' said Champion.

GLOSSARY

- **interrupted:** spoke while someone was speaking
- **on display:** where the public can see it
- **pleasure:** good feeling
- **put on:** showed
- **trap:** (here) plan to catch a person or an animal

'Exactly, Sir!' said Gabriel, 'Very dangerous. I think the Angel likes danger. The Angel is the best in the world, and he – or she – needs a new challenge•.'

Madame Helene laughed.

'Well, I don't care what this Angel needs, but they stole the Empress Josephine's ruby necklace. And I want it back! So, we will help you. Teddy can help with the details.' Madame Helene smiled at the detective, 'And I hope to see you soon, Detective.'

She turned and walked away. Teddy nodded his head at Sergeant Gabriel, then quickly followed her.

'Well, Sir?' asked Gabriel.

'You thought of this idea yourself?' asked Champion.

'Yes, Sir, I've studied every one of the Angel's thefts. I wrote a computer programme to try to understand them. Here...' Gabriel turned around his laptop to show the detective.

'I've worked out the danger and difficulty of each theft. I noticed that something has happened over the years. For the first ten years the level of difficulty and danger of the thefts was always the same. Then suddenly, ten years ago, each theft became more dangerous and difficult!' Gabriel sat back and looked at the detective.

Detective Champion did not have a laptop. He did not like computers. He liked to look people in the eye and know what they were thinking. And right now, he did not know what Gabriel was thinking. And he didn't like that.

'I understand. You have done your homework. Well done, Sergeant. So... a trap, tomorrow? Back at the Palais-Royal? Do you think you can do it?' asked Champion.

'Me, Sir? I thought you...'

'Oh, no, this is your work Gabriel, your excellent work. You make the trap. But I will arrest• the Angel. Do you understand?'

Gabriel nodded. 'I understand, Sir.'

• **arrest:** take someone to a police station • **challenge:** difficult test

Listen in

What do Madame Helene and Teddy say when they leave the police station? Listen, then do the activities.

1 **Listen and take notes about what Madame Helene and Teddy say about the following.**

	Madame Helene	Teddy
Detective Champion	not expectet	not catching Angel
The trap	not sure	clever idea
Things of value	Mona Lisa	golden things

2 **Listen again and tick (✓) true (T) or false (F).**

	T	F
a Madame Helene was surprised by Detective Champion.	☒	☐
b Madame Helene seems to trust Teddy.	☐	☒
c Madame Helene thinks art is more valuable than jewellery.	☒	☐

3 **In pairs, share your answers to Exercise 2. Give reasons for your answers.**

4 **Go to HELBLING e-zone to do the activities and get a clue to help you solve the mystery of the Angel.**

My clue is ....

5 Isabelle

Angelica was lying on the sofa watching an old movie when the doorbell rang. She didn't get up. It was 11 in the morning, and she felt very lazy. There were no emails, so no replacement Angel. Angelica didn't know what to do.

Porter stood in the doorway of the living room.

'Who is it, Porter?' asked Angelica.

'It is–' but before he could finish, someone ran into the room.

'ANGELICA!' a voice shouted. Angelica jumped up.

'Isabelle!' It was her niece. They hugged• and kissed each other on the cheeks. Angelica looked at her sister's daughter. She was taller than she remembered, and her hair was longer. But her eyes and smile were the same.

'What are you doing here? I thought you were at school in Switzerland!' asked Angelica.

Isabelle sat down on one of the big chairs.

'Umm, I was! But there was a gymnastics• competition in Marseilles, so I went home for a while. Then father said he was coming to Paris for some diplomatic thing•, so I came with him! It's nearly the Christmas holidays anyway, schoolwork is done for the year!'

GLOSSARY

- **diplomatic thing:** something that helps countries to communicate
- **gymnastics:** sport with physical exercises on the floor and on supports
- **hugged:** put their arms around each other

'Your bag, Miss Isabelle?' asked Porter. He was holding an old blue backpack in his hand.

'Umm yes... Angelica, can I stay here?' said Isabelle with a smile.

'Of course! But what about your father?' asked Angelica.

'I'll put your bag in the Blue Room, Miss Isabelle,' said Porter. 'And then I'll bring you some coffee.'

'Thank you, Porter,' said Angelica.

Porter turned away and took Isabelle's bag to one of the guest rooms.

'Father's staying in the government apartments.' Isabelle put her feet up over the edge of the chair and smiled. 'Ah it's good to be back here! I love your house. Have you sold lots of expensive art recently?'

Angelica looked at her niece. She wasn't a child anymore. Angelica's family thought she was an art dealer. No one, except Porter, knew who she really was. It was strange for Isabelle to suddenly arrive like this. She was 16 now, Angelica's age when she first met the Angel. Maybe it's a sign. But no, she couldn't put her family in danger.

'Oh a few things. The art world is quiet these days. No one appreciates the beauty of art. It's all technology and celebrities and bad news,' said Angelica.

'I love art! And technology, too. Did Mother tell you I'm a programmer now?' asked Isabelle.

'No, she didn't! Are you studying coding at school?'

'No, just for fun. It's all about languages and puzzles really – and I'm good at both!' she laughed.

It was true. When Isabelle was only 10 years old, she could speak perfect French, English, German, and Italian and she was even learning Chinese! It was good to see her niece again. She was full of life.

'So! Auntie Angel!' said Isabelle, 'Oh – thank you Porter!'

Porter arrived with two cups of coffee on a tray. He looked at Angelica and walked out.

'Oh please don't call me that!' laughed Angelica, 'It makes me sound so old!'

'Ha, sorry – Angelica... what are we doing today?'

They looked at each other for a second.

'Shopping!' they said together, and laughed.

'Oh yes, I've missed our Paris shopping trips, there's nothing cool to buy in Switzerland!' said Isabelle.

'Cool clothes aren't everything, Isabelle,' said Angelica.

'You can't say that!' said Isabelle laughing. It was true. Angelica loved shopping – not going from shop to shop – but the feeling of finding that perfect dress or top always made her feel happy.

GLOSSARY

- **appreciates:** sees the qualities of something
- **celebrities:** very famous people
- **coding:** writing computer programmes
- **I've missed:** I was sad because I wasn't there
- **top:** (here) t-shirt or shirt
- **tray:** 

Listen in

What do Angelica and Isabelle talk about when they go shopping? Listen, then do the activities.

1 Listen and tick (✓) who says the following.

a 'Busy, noisy and expensive.'
☐ Angelica ☐ Isabelle

b 'It was nearly two years ago.'
☐ Angelica ☐ Isabelle

c 'Time flies.'
☐ Angelica ☐ Isabelle

d 'You should try Switzerland.'
☐ Angelica ☐ Isabelle

e 'That's not true!'
☐ Angelica ☐ Isabelle

f 'Don't be silly!'
☐ Angelica ☐ Isabelle

2 Listen again. Then, with a partner, say what each one is referring to.

3 Go to HELBLING e-zone to do the activities and get a clue to help you solve the mystery of the Angel.

My clue is ....

6 An Email

They were walking by the side of the river Seine, looking at all the second-hand• book and magazine stalls•. It was one of Angelica's favourite places in Paris. It was getting cold, but looking at old books, she forgot about the weather. She chatted with an old book seller. He knew more about Paris than anyone.

Suddenly Isabelle came running over.

'Angelica!'

'What is it, Isabelle?' she asked.

'My father has just phoned! There's going to be a secret event at the Palais-Royal tomorrow night! He's going, and he thinks the prime minister will be there, and lots of other famous people, too! And he has invited us! How amazing is that?' Isabelle was very excited.

'The prime minister is going to the Palais-Royal? But there's nothing there,' said Angelica.

'He didn't tell me exactly, but I think he said something about a crown?' Isabelle took Angelica's arm as they walked down the path by the river.

GLOSSARY

- **second-hand:** not new
- **stalls:** tables where things are sold at markets

'A crown? Well, the most famous one is probably Louis XV's. But all the jewels were taken from it years ago. It's been 150 years since the crown was last complete. Maybe it's that one?' Angelica knew all about the crown, but Isabelle didn't need to know why.

'You really know your history, Angelica! I'm not interested in the crown, but the prime minister will be there, and lots of famous people, too. It'll be fun. We *have* to go!' Isabelle was very excited.

'OK, OK! Let's go! It's the perfect chance• to show off• our new clothes at least! I don't know how many famous people will be there. It sounds a little boring to me!' Actually•, Angelica was very interested in going. And finding out who invited Isabelle's father.

'I need to go back home and decide what to wear,' said Isabelle.

'For tomorrow?' asked Angelica.

'No! For tonight! I'm meeting some friends for dinner, then maybe we'll go dancing,' she said. 'Would you like to come?'

'Aha, no... not for me, thank you. But you go and have fun with your friends.' Angelica wanted to find out more about the Palais-Royal event. 'I'll call Porter to come and pick us up•.'

Back at the house, after Isabelle left, Angelica sat in her study and researched• everyone who knew about the crown.

Who has a connection to• Isabelle's father? she wondered•. *Or to me?*

She looked through the pictures of all the staff• at the Palais-Royal.

Aha! There's a familiar• face.

Oh, this is wonderful. What is he doing there?

Angelica laughed to herself.

As she was laughing, Porter walked in.

'Miss Angelica?' he asked.

'Yes, Porter? Is everything OK?'

GLOSSARY

- **actually:** in truth; really
- **chance:** (here) opportunity; event
- **familiar:** that she knows
- **has a connection to:** (here) knows
- **pick us up:** (here) collect/get us (in a car)
- **researched:** studied
- **show off:** (here) show in public
- **staff:** people who work in a place
- **wondered:** asked herself

'Yes, Miss, but I am worried about Isabelle. She's a little too young to be going out alone in Paris. Do you want me to follow her?' asked Porter.

'She's 16 and she's with friends, Porter, I'm sure she'll be fine. But, if you don't mind•, could you stay up a bit later tonight? Just in case she needs a driver,' asked Angelica.

'Of course, Miss. And one more thing... do you really need to find a new Angel?'

Angelica paused. She really liked Porter. He would do anything to help her. *Would he like the next Angel? Would he want to work for him or her?* she wondered.

'I promised the first Angel,' she said. 'He was very special.'

'Yes, Miss, yes he was,' said Porter. He stopped talking.

'What is it, Porter?' asked Angelica. She knew him well.

'Something is different this time, Miss. I've done some research on the police.'

'Old Champion? I think we know all about him!' answered Angelica.

'No, Miss, this new sergeant, Gabriel. There's something about him. I'm not sure what, but I'd like to keep an eye on him.' It was strange for Porter to worry about the police.

'I see. Maybe I am getting too lazy. He could be someone to watch. OK Porter, you know what to do. I'll do some research, too. Thank you,' she smiled at her old friend.

'You're always welcome, Miss,' Porter turned and left the study.

Suddenly, her computer beeped. Angelica looked at the screen.

An email at last! Someone has solved my puzzle!

• **if you don't mind:** if it's not a problem for you

Listen in

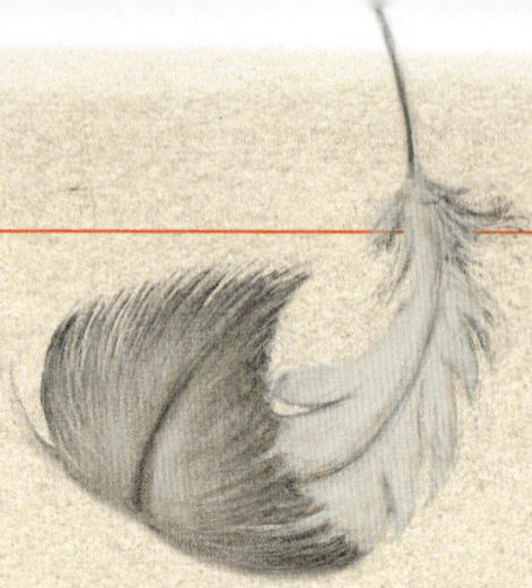

What is written in the email? Listen, then do the activities.

1 Listen and tick (✓) why the person wrote the email (there may be more than one correct answer).

a ☐ to discover who the Angel is
b ☐ to help the Angel to steal things
c ☐ to show s/he has solved the puzzle
d ☐ to do some other tests

2 Listen again and complete the email.

Dear **a** ...friend..., if you are reading this, you know I have solved your little **b** ...test...! It was very interesting. I love puzzles and tests. I would like to find out what other **c** ...answers... you have. But I will not **d** ...steal... things for you. I am not your assistant. I want to find out **e** ...who... you are and what other tests you have ready for me. Perhaps one day we can **f** ...work... together. First, your clue: 'The path to Victory lies in the wings. The Sport of Art is the way' was very **g** ...clever... . But I think there is more – what is victory? If you have something very valuable to **h** ...offer... me – then I am listening.
Yours,
The Problem Solver

3 Go to HELBLING e-zone to do the activities and get a clue to help you solve the mystery of the Angel.

My clue is ....

7 The Final Test

Angelica sat in shock. *It's really happening! Someone has solved the puzzle... Finally! I've dreamt about this moment for the last two years.* She opened a drawer in her desk, and pulled out the file on the final test. She wanted to make sure that everything was still in place, that each piece of jewellery was still in the same museum.

Angelica smiled. Only the best thieves could complete this test. She had a list of five pieces of jewellery: an amethyst ring, a nephrite jade brooch, a garnet necklace, a pair of emerald earrings, and a lapis lazuli bracelet. They were all from different periods• in history, and all in different museums across Paris. The first part of the test was to steal them all, in only 48 hours. *Difficult, but not impossible,* thought Angelica. But, of course, if anyone sees her – or him – that's it. They fail• the test. But if they succeed, then they have to bring the five pieces of jewellery to Angelica. And they have to tell her what they mean. The final part of the test.

GLOSSARY

- **fail:** not succeed
- **periods:** times

She spent a long time writing the email to the new thief. She wanted to give clear instructions•, but not to help *too* much. When she was happy with it, she sent the email. And now she wanted to find out more about the thief. Her email had another secret. A tracker• virus. *When the new thief opens the email, I'll know where she – or he – is!* She waited and watched. Nothing happened. She went to get some water from the kitchen.

When she came back, still nothing. What was happening? Then her computer beeped. A reply from the new thief! But there was no information about where he or she was! Angelica clapped• her hands and laughed. This person was very clever! She – or he – blocked• the virus. Brilliant! Maybe this really was the one. Angelica felt happier than she had felt in a long time.

GLOSSARY

- **blocked:** stopped
- **clapped:** put together (to make a sound because she was happy)
- **instructions:** things to do to complete something
- **tracker:** (here) that shows where someone is

She turned off her computer and the lights, then she went upstairs to her bedroom. She lay in bed but couldn't sleep. *Is my life as the Angel really going to be over•?* She thought about Isabelle. She hoped she was having a good time with her friends. Angelica got up and opened a window for some fresh air. Looking down into her garden, she heard voices. Porter? Yes, she could see him in the light from the kitchen window. He was talking to a woman. One of his contacts. Porter had contacts all over Paris. Very useful for getting information. Porter was very important to Angelica. *What is he going to do without me?* she wondered. *And what am I going to do without him?*

In the morning Angelica woke up feeling tired, but she was in a good mood•. Things were happening, and sometimes change was for the better. 'Think of change as an old friend,' that's what the first Angel always said. He was right. Change was her friend.

She went downstairs to the kitchen. Isabelle and Porter were talking. Isabelle was eating an omelette•.

'Auntie!' she said, 'I was telling Porter I had such a good evening! Oh, I've missed Paris... the music... the people!'

Angelica smiled and yawned•.

'Coffee, Miss,' said Porter, and gave her a large cup.

Angelica sat down at the big kitchen table.

'So, Isabelle, what are we doing today?' she asked.

Isabelle finished her omelette, and sat back in her chair.

'Umm... I'm going to go back to bed, I think. Sorry Angelica!' she stood up and left the room. 'Wake me up this afternoon!'

Angelica looked at Porter.

'Teenagers,' she said. Porter smiled, and then looked serious.

'Miss, I have some information on the new police sergeant,' he said.

'Aha. And I have some information on an old friend. I think we have lots to plan today, Porter.'

- **be over:** finish; end
- **mood:** how she feels
- **omelette:** meal with eggs
- **yawned:** opened her mouth because she was tired

Listen in

What does Porter say to his contact? Listen, then do the activities.

1 Listen and put the things that Jeanne does in order.

a ☐ She waited outside the police station.
b ☐ She changed into a cleaner's uniform.
c ☐ Then she went inside.
d ☐ Then she followed Sergeant Gabriel.
e ☐ She went to the police station.
f ☐ She cleaned the floor of the police station.
g ☐ She lost Sergeant Gabriel
h ☐ She left the police station.
i ☐ She saw him looking out of his window.
j ☐ She went into the bathroom.

2 Jeanne tells a lie, what is it? Tell a friend.

3 Go to HELBLING e-zone to do the activities and get a clue to help you solve the mystery of the Angel.

My clue is ....

8 At the Palais-Royal

'Detective Champion, welcome!'

The detective was standing in one of the many entrance halls• in the Palais-Royal. Coming towards him was Madame Helene, the Head of Exhibitions. She looked very glamorous•. She had her usual vintage glasses on, but this evening she was wearing a long white dress and lots of jewellery.

She held out her arm and they walked into the main• reception room• together.

'It is good to see you again, Madame,' said the detective.

'Oh, please! Call me Helene,' she smiled. 'Your sergeant Gabriel has been very busy organising our little...' she paused, and looked around, 'trap! It's very exciting! A chance to catch this famous thief.'

Detective Champion looked at the entrance to the room. There were four guards and a metal detector• in the doorway. He saw three cameras inside the door and two more outside. The security• looked good.

'So, Gabriel told you all about the Angel?' he said.

GLOSSARY

- **glamorous:** beautiful and elegant
- **halls:** (here) large rooms
- **main:** most important
- **metal detector:** machine to find metal
- **reception room:** room for events and parties
- **security:** system to keep a place safe

'Yes, a little. And my assistant, Teddy, knows a lot about the Angel, too. I didn't know he was so famous! And if we catch him, well you and I will be famous too, Detective, don't you think so?' Madame Helene looked very excited.

The detective tried to look serious and professional.

'It's all in a day's work, Madame – I mean Helene – catching criminals is what I do. I have no need to be famous!'

'Well, I am sure you will be famous, Detective, absolutely sure. Now... some important information, have you heard that the prime minister is coming?' she said as they walked into the main entrance.

It was already quite busy. Groups of people in designer clothes were walking around the palace halls, quietly talking. The detective looked at his watch – 8 p.m. The crown was going on display in exactly one hour, in a private room underground.

'Yes, I heard, Gabriel is talking with his security team. We have to be very careful. The Angel is dangerous!'

'Oh, really, Detective! I think with you here, we are all very safe.' She smiled at him.

They continued walking through the halls, past the richest and most powerful people of Paris. The detective looked at each one of them very carefully. Any one of them could be the Angel. Except the prime minister. Maybe.

'And here is the underground room where we will show the crown.' Madame Helene pointed to some stairs which went down to double doors. There were two more security guards at the top of the stairs, and two more cameras on the walls.

'Excellent,' said the detective.

They walked down the stairs and opened the doors. Inside was a large room. At one end was a silver• box with a glass case on top and two security guards at its sides. It was covered with a red cloth. Above the box were two very bright lights, and around it were alarms with lasers. There were cameras at each end of the room, and in front of the box were chairs for the guests•. Two of these chairs had people sitting on them – Sergeant Gabriel and Helene's assistant, Teddy. Teddy was wearing a dark red suit and an orange tie.

'Sir!' said Gabriel, jumping up from his chair, 'As you can see, everything is ready. There is only one way in and out of this room – that door.'

The detective looked around the room. He carefully examined• the ceiling, the walls and the floor. He looked very carefully at the two guards on either side of the box.

'I can promise you, Detective, the room is perfectly safe,' said Teddy. 'There is no way the Angel can take the crown out of this room!'

'Yes, I see. But isn't it *too* difficult? If the Angel has no chance, how do we know he will try to take the crown?' asked the detective.

'The Angel is the best of the best, Sir,' said Gabriel.

'Ah yes, but, not for long,' said Teddy, laughing to himself.

'Well, Detective, I'm sorry I have to leave you now and go and meet my guests! It's wonderful to see you, and good luck this evening... it's all so exciting!' Madame Helene turned and walked out of the room and up the stairs. 'Come on, Teddy!' she shouted behind her.

Teddy smiled at the detective.

'Tonight is going to be special,' he said, and followed Helene.

GLOSSARY

- **examined:** carefully looked at
- **guests:** people invited to an event
- **silver:** precious white metal

Listen in

What do the security guards say about the event? Listen, then do the activities.

1 **Listen, then read the newspaper article. Circle the false statements.**

LOUIS XV's CROWN ON SHOW

Louis XV's 200-year-old crown goes on show at the Louvre this evening.

The crown, which was made in 1822, is famous for its beautiful glass jewels, including a copy of the Regent diamond. The Regent diamond was stolen by the Angel, last year.

2 **Listen again. With a partner, correct the false statements.**

3 **Go to HELBLING e-zone to do the activities and get a clue to help you solve the mystery of the Angel.**

My clue is ....

9 Teddy

Angelica sat on the steps of the grand staircase in her home, and waited. She looked up at Porter. He was waiting patiently by the front door.

'ISABELLE!' she shouted. There was no answer. How long did it take her niece to get ready? 'It's nearly 8! We need to go!' she shouted again. Still no answer. Angelica stood up. She lifted the silk of her long grey dress above her shoes, and walked over to Porter.

'Are we ready for this evening, Porter?' she asked.

'Yes, Miss. My friends are watching everything.'

'Do you really think he'll try to kidnap• me tonight?' she asked.

'I don't know, Miss. You never know with him. But yes, there was a room in the house ready to keep someone prisoner•,' he replied.

'What a strange thing to do,' Angelica sighed•. But things were going well, and she didn't feel worried. *Tonight is going to be fun*, she thought.

'Sorry!' came a voice from upstairs. Isabelle came quickly but carefully down the stairs in her high heels•.

GLOSSARY

- **heels:** high part in shoes
- **keep someone prisoner:** force someone to stay in a place
- **kidnap:** take a person and ask for something to free them
- **sighed:** made a loud noise when breathing (when worried or sad)

She was wearing a long red dress and a small diamond necklace.

'Thank you for the necklace! It's beautiful!' she said.

'You're very welcome. And you look amazing! I can't believe how much you've grown up•,' said Angelica.

'I feel like I'm going to a ball•!' said Isabelle.

'Well, don't get too excited – it's just a lot of boring rich people looking at an old crown,' said Angelica.

'Oh, anything can happen!' laughed Isabelle.

Porter opened the door, and they went down to the car that was waiting outside.

They drove through the streets of Paris, and soon arrived at the Palais-Royal. They went through the security checkpoints• and into the main reception room.

There were musicians playing classical music, and waiters carrying trays of champagne and food. Everyone looked very glamorous.

'This is amazing!' said Isabelle. 'I'm going to find father – he must be here somewhere!' She walked away through the groups of people in the beautiful old palace.

Angelica walked slowly through the hallways, looking at the old paintings and the people. She couldn't see the prime minister. But she was looking for someone else – she knew he was here. *He'll show himself soon, I'm sure.*

She checked her watch. 8.50 p.m.

Just ten minutes to go•.

She was looking at a painting of a horse when a man appeared next to her. He was wearing a dark red suit with an orange tie. She didn't look at him.

'Terence. The Phoenix. So, you have returned to Paris?' she said.

'Ah, you remember me! After ten years... but it's not Terence. You can call me Teddy now,' he said and smiled. Her old friend. Her old enemy. The man who wanted to be the Angel but failed the test.

'You're not still angry, are you, Terence?' asked Angelica.

GLOSSARY

- **ball:** formal dance
- **checkpoints:** places where police check people
- **grown up:** (usually of children) become adult and mature
- **to go:** (here) before the event started

'Angry?! No! Why would I be angry? I was the better thief, we all knew that. But the Angel wanted you. It was a popularity• contest. Not a real competition!' he said.

'The police saw you,' she said.

Teddy's face became red.

'Once! And they didn't see my face!' Teddy took a deep breath. 'And anyway it doesn't matter•. The police know you are here to take the crown.'

'Oh, I know,' Angelica smiled.

'Ha! And you don't care! You always thought you were better than everyone!'

'But what are you doing here, Ter–Teddy?' asked Angelica.

'Me? I'm working! This is my job now. I'm not a thief. I don't take other people's things. I work, I live an honest life, not like some people I know. I'm going to watch you tonight!' he said, and walked away.

Angelica smiled to herself. *He'll never change*, she thought. She saw that everyone was moving in the same direction – to the underground room. It was time to see the crown.

As she came to the top of the steps, a tall slim man with short dark hair stood in front of her.

'Oh! I'm so sorry, Mademoiselle, after you•,' he said.

Angelica smiled. He was very handsome. And she knew exactly who he was.

'No, please, Sergeant, after you...'

'Oh no, please, ladies first – wait – did you just call me Sergeant?' Sergeant Gabriel's face was very surprised. Angelica wanted to laugh, but she did not. Instead, she took his arm and walked quickly down the stairs.

'I think the show is about to begin,' she said.

- **after you:** (here) you go first
- **it doesn't matter:** it isn't important
- **popularity:** quality of being liked by many people

Listen in

What does Teddy say to Isabelle? Listen, then do the activities.

1 Listen. What happens during the dialogue?

a ☐ Teddy asks Isabelle about her aunt, Angelica.
b ☐ Teddy takes Isabelle to her father.
c ☐ Teddy threatens Isabelle and ties her up.
d ☐ Teddy makes a business proposal to Isabelle.

2 Listen again. How does Isabelle react when Teddy says the following things?

a 'Your father asked me to find you.'
b 'I have a gun.'
c 'Now, sit on the chair.'
d 'She (your aunt) and I have unfinished business to solve.'

3 What does this tell us about Isabelle? Would you react in the same way?

4 Go to HELBLING e-zone to do the activities and get a clue to help you solve the mystery of the Angel.

My clue is ....

10 The Crown

'But who are you?' whispered• Gabriel. It was quiet in the underground room, nearly all the seats were taken.

'A friend,' Angelica replied. 'And I think someone is looking for you.' She pointed ahead.

Detective Champion was sitting in the front row, staring• at Gabriel.

'I–' said Gabriel, but Angelica turned away to look for Isabelle. Gabriel watched her for a second, then went to sit next to the detective and Madame Helene. Teddy was standing at the side of the room.

Angelica looked around, she could see the prime minister at the front with his security team. And there was Marc, Isabelle's father. He smiled at her and Angelica waved• back. But she couldn't see Isabelle. Where was she? Why wasn't she with her father? Angelica took out her phone. There was no signal• here.

Madame Helene went up to the front of the room. Angelica quickly sat down.

'Ladies and gentlemen! Friends and guests! And of course, our wonderful prime minister! Welcome to the Palais-Royal,' she said. Everyone in the room clapped politely.

GLOSSARY

- **signal:** (of mobile phones) ability to make phone calls
- **staring:** looking in a fixed way
- **waved:** moved her hand from side to side (to say 'hello')
- **whispered:** said quietly

'This was the home of the royal family for a very long time. And we are lucky today to see a very important piece of French history, the crown of Louis XV! Now, for the first time in many years, the crown is complete with the famous Regent diamond.'

Madame Helene took the red cover from the glass case. *How beautiful!* thought Angelica. Everyone clapped and cheered•. Except for three people. They did not look very happy at all.

Teddy, also known as Terence, the Phoenix, was surprised to see the crown there. That spoiled• his plan. But it wasn't a problem, as he had another one.

Detective Champion was angry, too. Why didn't the trap work? Where was the Angel?

Sergeant Gabriel was a little embarrassed•. He was sure something would happen so the Angel could take the crown! But – nothing.

Madame Helene smiled at the room. 'And now, ladies and gentlemen, please come up and take a closer look at the crown!'

The room was noisy as people stood up and moved around. Angelica stayed at the back and looked for Isabelle. Then she suddenly felt cold as she thought of something. *Terence isn't going to kidnap me... It's Isabelle he wants!* Terence – her old enemy. But kidnapping a young girl! She was angry. Very angry. However, Angelica still had her plan. And her plans never failed.

GLOSSARY

- **cheered:** shouted in happiness
- **embarrassed:** (here) uncomfortable (because something didn't happen)
- **spoiled:** (here) stopped from working

She left the room quickly. She didn't want Isabelle's father to know what was happening. She called Isabelle's mobile phone. It went to voicemail•. She called Porter.

'Porter!' she said.

'Miss? I thought Terence was going to kidnap you,' said the voice through the phone.

'Yes, I thought so, too. But I was wrong. He took Isabelle.'

Porter was silent.

'What do we do, Miss?' he asked.

'Don't hurt him, Porter. We keep to the plan. We thought he was going to kidnap me, and we prepared for that. Now he has Isabelle, but they are still in the building. He was at the ceremony•, but I don't know where he put Isabelle. But we know where he is going to take her. Follow him. He will call me later, and I will go to meet him. When he leaves, you can free Isabelle.' Angelica was calm on the outside, but inside she was very angry.

'I understand, Miss,' said Porter.

'Thank you,' she answered quietly.

Angelica walked outside into the cold night air. She hoped that Isabelle was OK. Her niece probably thought it was all very exciting. There was another thought, one that Angelica didn't like to think about – what if the person who solved her puzzle, was Isabelle?

'Excuse me,' said a voice behind her. It was Sergeant Gabriel.

'Yes, Sergeant,' she said.

The tall policeman smiled at her.

'You left very quickly. Don't you want to see the crown, Miss...?'

'"Miss" is fine. Oh, I think crowns all look the same. Not a very interesting evening was it?' she said.

'Actually, I think it was very interesting,' he said. 'Sometimes we learn more when nothing happens.'

Angelica smiled. He was right.

'Good night, Gabriel,' she said, and walked away into the night.

- **ceremony:** formal event
- **voicemail:** phone answering service

Listen in

What do Detective Champion and Sergeant Gabriel say after the event? Listen, then do the activities.

1 Listen and tick (✓) true (T), false (F) or don't know (D).

	T	F	D
a Sergeant Gabriel's plan didn't work.	☐	☐	☐
b The Angel was present at the event.	☐	☐	☐
c The crown is safe.	☐	☐	☐
d They know how to catch the Angel now.	☐	☐	☐
e Detective Champion is going home.	☐	☐	☐
f Sergeant Gabriel is going home.	☐	☐	☐

2 Listen again. Find evidence of the following statements. Share your ideas in pairs.

a Sergeant Gabriel thinks the Angel was at the event.

b Detective Champion isn't happy with Sergeant Gabriel.

c Sergeant Gabriel didn't think it would be easy to catch the Angel.

3 Go to HELBLING e-zone to do the activities and get a clue to help you solve the mystery of the Angel.

My clue is ....

11 Paris by Night

Later that evening, Angelica walked up and down the collection of glass cases in her secret room. She looked at each one of the beautiful pieces of jewellery, but she couldn't stop thinking about Isabelle.

Porter and his contacts watched Terence the Phoenix put Isabelle into his car at the Palais-Royal after the event, and then they watched him drive her to a small house just outside Paris. They told her that Isabelle seemed fine. She was a strong girl. And Terence had no idea that Angelica knew exactly what he was doing.

But when was he going to call? She stopped by two glass cases. One was now empty – that item was now in a secret place. All part of her plan.

She went back to her study and closed the secret door. Just then, her phone rang. She looked down – unknown number. Ha! He thought he could hide from her.

She answered.

'ANGEL,' said a voice. It sounded like a robot.

'Who is this?' she said, trying to seem worried.

'I HAVE YOUR NIECE. SHE IS SAFE. IF YOU WANT TO SEE HER AGAIN, DO WHAT I SAY.'

Angelica smiled.

'Oh no! Where is she?! Is she OK? What have you done to her?' she said.

'DO NOT WORRY. I KNOW WHO YOU ARE. I KNOW WHAT YOU DO. BRING ALL YOUR JEWELS TO THE FOUNTAINS IN THE TROCADERO GARDENS. LEAVE THEM THERE. THEN YOU WILL SEE YOUR NIECE AGAIN.'

'I don't know what you mean! I sell art! I don't have any jewels...' Angelica tried very hard to seem scared, but she had to cover her mouth to stop laughing.

'NO GAMES,• ANGEL. BE THERE TONIGHT AT 1 A.M.' He hung up•.

Angelica could finally laugh. Oh Terence! What a silly man. He really did think he was a phoenix, rising up• again, but instead, he was just an angry man. Still angry after all these years. Unless... *could he have solved my puzzle? He is intelligent, after all. What if this is all a game? He just wants to prove that he is as good as me.* Angelica thought about this for a while. Well, there was still the final part of the test to complete. The person who sent the email needed to steal the five pieces of jewellery and bring them to her, before it was too late.

GLOSSARY

- **hung up:** stopped the call
- **no games:** don't do anything strange
- **rising up:** (here) coming to life

It was time to get ready. *Terence will come to the gardens himself,* Angelica thought. *He won't let anyone else touch the jewels. And he won't bring Isabelle to the gardens. That's too dangerous. He'll call me later and tell me where to find her.*

It was all going to work out perfectly.

She took a big backpack, and filled it carefully with all the jewellery from her collection. All except one piece. That one she kept. It would be a gift for the new Angel. Finally, she opened a drawer in her desk, and took out a small black circle. It was a GPS-tracker. With it, she could follow the jewellery anywhere in the world. She carefully hid the tracker in Empress Josephine's ruby necklace.

Angelica went down to the garage. She kept her motorbike there. It was bright red and beautiful and very fast. She put on her jacket, boots and helmet. It was half past twelve. She put on the heavy backpack full of jewellery and turned the key. The engine roared to life. The garage door opened automatically, and she rode her motorbike out into the cold streets. She loved riding around the streets at night. It made her feel free.

She rode through the traffic. Paris was always busy, but on her bike she arrived quickly at the gardens. She parked on a small side street and walked down to an old pay phone.

It was time to call the police.

She left a message for Detective Champion. It was the least she could do. It was only fair for him to be the one to catch... the Angel.

She smiled to herself. This was going to be fun.

- **helmet:** 
- **roared to life:** started noisily
- **side street:** small street that goes onto a bigger one
- **work out:** (here) finish; be solved

Listen in

What does Angelica say in her message to Detective Champion? Listen, then do the activities.

1 Listen and write phrases from the audio track to match the sentences below.

a I'm afraid he's not available at the moment.

b Do you know something about the Angel?

c Could you give me your full name, please.

d That seems very strange.

2 Listen again. What information does Angelica give the police?

3 Do you think the information is true? Discuss with a partner.

4 Go to HELBLING e-zone to do the activities and get a clue to help you solve the mystery of the Angel.

My clue is ....

12 The Gardens

Angelica walked around the gardens silently, like a ghost. She had to make sure they were empty, and that no one else• took the bag. She knew that Terence was waiting somewhere nearby. And that the police were on their way. She hoped that the detective received her message in time. Porter should be with Isabelle now, too. And Terence had no idea!

Angelica stepped out into the light from a lamppost• and on to the main path. The fountains were in front of her. They were off• now, there was only a silent pool of water. She walked forward and put her backpack down on the ground. It was only ten to one.

Ten years of her life. Ten years of amazing thefts. All in this one backpack. Well, not all. One piece was still at her home.

Angelica took one last look around the gardens. Then she walked quickly away into the trees, and disappeared. But she didn't leave. She wanted to watch what happened.

GLOSSARY

- **lamppost:** 
- **no one else:** no other person
- **off:** (here) not working

Soon she saw someone appear. It was a man in a tracksuit•. A jogger• – clever! It was Terence of course. But where were the police?

Suddenly, she felt her phone ring. Porter. He spoke quickly. Isabelle was safe! And they were nearly home. The first part of the plan was going well.

She watched Terence pick up• the backpack full of jewellery. He looked around carefully. There was no one there. *How could the police be late tonight?!* thought Angelica.

Terence put the backpack on and started running away. He was slow – all the jewellery made the backpack very heavy.

Then she heard the police sirens! At last! Blue lights came flashing around the park. Two, three, four cars! They stopped, and lots of policemen ran into the park. But Terence was already running down

GLOSSARY

- **jogger:** person who runs for sport
- **pick up:** lift; take in his hands
- **tracksuit:** 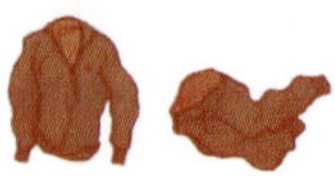

another road. Angelica moved so she could see what was happening. He was running towards his car. She saw him jump in and start the engine. Then one of the policemen saw him and shouted.

More police cars were coming. Terence drove quickly into the road and spun• the car around. He raced• away from the police. How exciting! Angelica stood up and walked to the edge of the gardens. Five police cars were chasing Terence down the road. And there was Detective Champion! She could see him driving.

He looked very excited.

Her work was done. *They will catch him,* she thought. *Or, if they don't, I've put the GPS tracker in the necklace. The police will know where he is.*

Angelica went back to her motorbike, put her helmet on, and rode home. She was smiling all the way.

As soon as she came home, she ran upstairs. She could hear voices in the kitchen. Isabelle was talking to Porter.

'Isabelle!'

- **raced:** went very quickly
- **spun:** quickly turned in a circle

'Oh Angelica! I had such a fun time,' Isabelle jumped up to hug Angelica.

'Fun? You were kidnapped!' said Angelica.

'Well yes... but I was never in danger. I knew that you and Porter were watching me. I'm never in danger with you. You're my angel,' she said and smiled at her aunt.

'But I'm a little tired! I think I'll go to bed. Father is coming to pick me up early tomorrow morning. Thank you for a wonderful evening,' said Isabelle, and put down her tea. 'And thank you Porter, you are my hero,' she kissed him on the cheek, and went upstairs.

'That girl – how is she so brave?' said Angelica.

'I don't know, Miss, but maybe she knows more about you than you think,' said Porter.

'Yes, you could be right. Well done tonight, Porter.' Angelica smiled at him and went back downstairs to her study.

She sat down and turned on her laptop. There was just one last thing left to do.

Aha! There it was. The email from the new thief. Test completed! And in only 24 hours. Now that was very impressive•. This new thief was someone special. She – or he – stole all five pieces of jewellery and guessed the hidden meaning, too.

It was over. It was time for a new Angel. She replied to the email with her address and instructions to come at 9 the following morning. The only question was... who was the new Angel?

GLOSSARY

- **impressive:** amazing; extraordinary

After Reading

Over to you

1 **Can you solve the mystery of the Angel? First, write your clues below.**

2 **Now look at the pictures and choose the new Angel.**

3 **Now tell a friend, explaining why.**

4 **Listen and check.**

After Reading

Listen in and Think

1 Listen and choose the correct answer to each question.

a Who is in the house with Angelica?
1 ☐ Isabelle
2 ☐ Porter
3 ☐ Isabelle's father

b Who solved Angelica's puzzle?
1 ☐ Sergeant Gabriel
2 ☐ Porter
3 ☐ Isabelle

c Why is it strange that Detective Champion caught the Angel?
1 ☐ because Gabriel has the ruby necklace
2 ☐ because the case was too difficult
3 ☐ because Teddy isn't the Angel

d Why does Gabriel think that Teddy is not the Angel?
1 ☐ He didn't have all the jewellery.
2 ☐ He isn't clever enough.
3 ☐ Detective Champion isn't happy.

e What did the owner do when he caught Angelica and Terence in his house?
1 ☐ He called the police.
2 ☐ He taught them to be better thieves.
3 ☐ He sent them to boarding school.

f What was Angelica's final task from the original Angel?
1 ☐ to steal a Van Gogh painting
2 ☐ to ask Terence to be her guardian
3 ☐ to find a new Angel

g Where was the secret door?
1 ☐ under the desk
2 ☐ in the bookcase
3 ☐ behind the glass case

2 Listen to the author, Gavin Biggs, talking about *The Angel*. Then choose the correct answer.

a Who is Gavin's favourite character?
1 ☐ Isabelle
2 ☐ Angelica
3 ☐ Gabriel

b How is Gavin like Gabriel?
1 ☐ They are both cool.
2 ☐ They both like to learn new things.
3 ☐ They both like to travel.

c How does Gavin describe books about jewel thieves?
1 ☐ cool, dangerous and important
2 ☐ exciting, intelligent and dangerous
3 ☐ modern, mysterious and brilliant

d When did Agatha Christie stop writing?
1 ☐ 1920s
2 ☐ 1940s
3 ☐ 1970s

3 Listen again. Then answer the questions with a friend.

a Why is Angelica Gavin's favourite character?
b What do you think Angelica does next?
c Who is your favourite author?

4 In pairs, answer the following questions. Give reasons for your answers.

a Who was your favourite character?
b What was your favourite chapter?
c Why did Angelica retire as the Angel?
d Will Gabriel be a good Angel?

After Reading

Vocabulary

1 Complete the word groups with the words from the story.

amethyst bracelet bronze brooch crown earrings emerald ~~garnet~~ gold jade necklace ring silver statue box diamond ruby

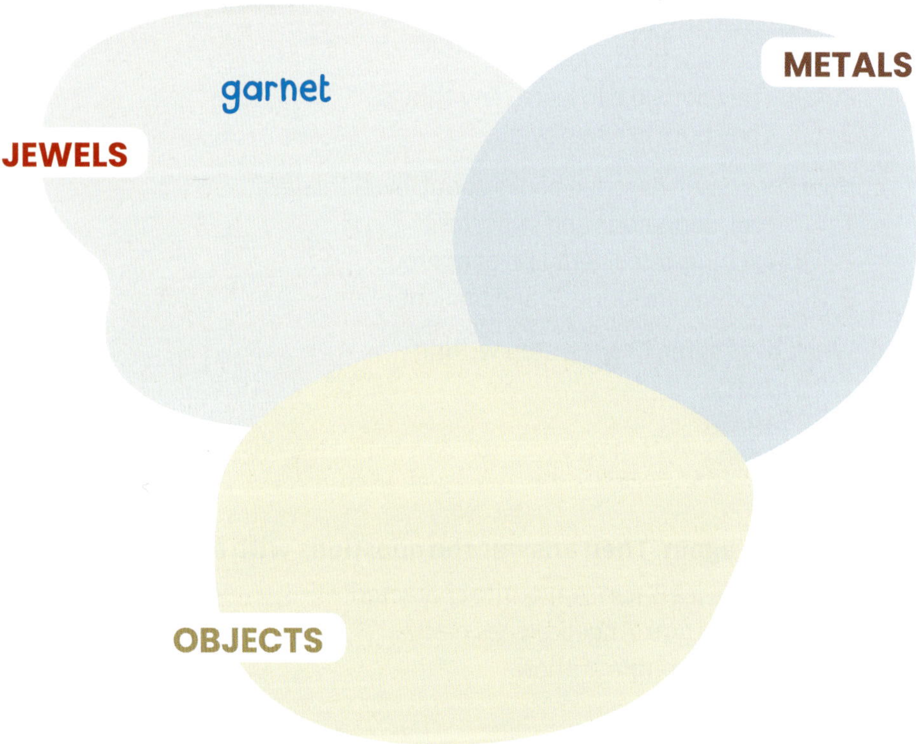

2 Match the precious jewels or metals to their colours.

a ☐ diamond
b ☐ ruby
c ☐ emerald
d ☐ bronze
e ☐ silver
f ☐ amethyst

1
2
3
4
5
6

3 **Label the pictures using two words from Exercise 1.**

a ....

....

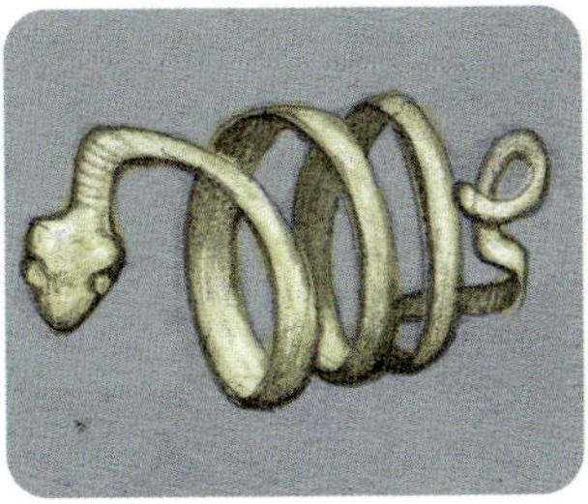

b ....

....

c ....

....

d ....

....

Listen in

4 **Listen to the pronunciation of the names of two of the main characters in the story. Pay attention to the underlined part of the word.**

a Angelica. The Angel.

b Detective Champion.

5 **With a partner, say these words aloud. Tick (✓) the words with the same sound as the middle part of *angel*. Put a cross (✗) next to the words with the same sound as the first part of *champion*.**

a ☐ Chinese **c** ☐ Japanese **e** ☐ kitchen **g** ☐ picture

b ☐ fridge **d** ☐ job **f** ☐ large **h** ☐ rich

6 **Listen and check.**

After Reading

Characters

1 Answer the questions with the name of a character.

a Who was a master of Chinese chess? ....

b Who stole a Van Gogh painting? ....

c Who goes to school in Switzerland? ....

d Who is described as a 'traditional policeman'? ....

e Who is the Head of Exhibitions at the Palais-Royal? ....

f Whose nickname is 'the Phoenix'? ....

g Who made a promise to protect Angelica? ....

h Who was Porter in love with many years ago? ....

2 In pairs, find evidence in the story to support the statements below. How do we know that…

- Gabriel loves solving problems?
- Angelica is good at climbing?
- Isabelle is calm in dangerous situations?
- Teddy is angry with Angelica?

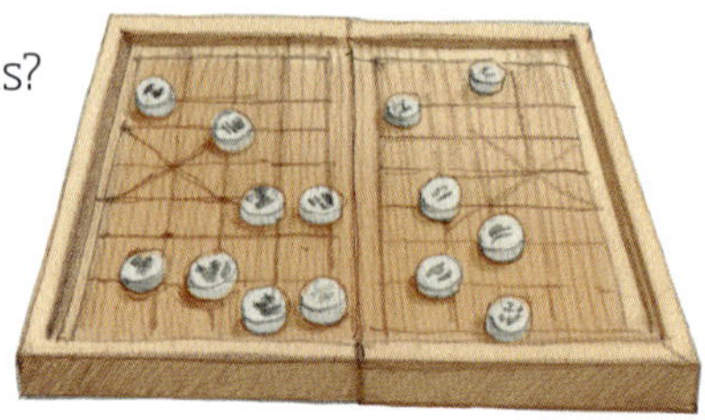

3 Complete the table with the information about the characters.

angry bald brave dangerous kind long hair loyal spiky hair teenager

TEDDY	PORTER	ISABELLE

4 Listen to the quotes from the story. Who is speaking?

a ....
b ....
c ....
d ....
e ....
f ....

5 Who were the characters speaking to in Exercise 4?

a ....
b ....
c ....
d ....
e ....
f ....

6 What do you think? Why is Angelica a better thief than Teddy? Discuss with a friend.

I think...

After Reading

Language

1 Match the phrasal verbs to their meanings.

a ☐ find out	1 stop trying
b ☐ give up	2 start (an alarm)
c ☐ carry out	3 stop a phone call
d ☐ put down	4 place something on the floor or a surface
e ☐ set off	5 learn some information
f ☐ show off	6 display something you are proud of
g ☐ hang up	7 do

2 Use the correct form of a phrasal verb from Exercise 1 to complete the sentences below.

a *How many years is it now?* she asked herself. *He'll never* .... *– but he'll never catch me!*

b 'Thank you for a wonderful evening,' said Isabelle and .... her tea.

c Ten years of planning and .... the most difficult and dangerous thefts.

d 'That's the only way to get to the necklace, without .... the alarm.'

e 'NO GAMES, ANGEL. BE THERE TONIGHT AT 1 A.M.' He ....

f 'OK, OK! Let's go! It's the perfect chance to .... our new clothes at least!'

g Angelica wanted to .... more about the Palais-Royal event.

h Detective Champion was an excellent investigator. He never .... He looked at every clue.

i 'What is that noise now!?'
'It's the alarm sir. Errr.... We .... it ....'

3 Listen and check.

4 **Complete the sentences below with *too* and an adjective from the box. There are three extra words.**

amazing dangerous difficult excited expensive late strong young

a The person who sent the email needed to steal the five pieces of jewellery and bring them to her, before it was ....
b He won't let anyone else touch the jewels. And he won't bring Isabelle to the gardens. That's ....
c Were her puzzles ....? No, she needed someone clever.
d 'Yes, Miss, but I am worried about Isabelle. She's a little .... to be going out alone in Paris.'
e 'Well, don't get .... – it's just a lot of boring rich people looking at an old crown,' said Angelica.

5 **Listen and check.**

6 **Write three of your own sentences using *too* and words from the box below.**

easy lazy tired

a ....
b ....
c ....

7 **Use the correct form of the verb in brackets to form the present perfect.**

a 'An email at last! Someone .... my puzzle!' (solve)
b 'Terence isn't here. He .... back home.' (go)
c 'My father .... us to a special event at the Palais-Royal!' (invite)
d 'Terence. The Phoenix. So, you .... to Paris?' (return)
e 'We .... all the original stones, including the famous Regent diamond.' (find)

After Reading

Plot

1 What happens in the story? Put the sentences in the correct order.

1	2	3	4	5	6	7	8	9	10	11	12
f											

a Someone solved Angelica's puzzle.
b Louis XV's famous crown went on display at the Palais-Royal.
c Angelica told Gabriel her story.
d Detective Champion closed the case of the Angel.
e Madame Helene met Detective Champion for the first time.
f Angelica stole the Empress Josephine's ruby necklace.
g Teddy found the backpack full of jewellery next to the fountains.
h Angelica rode her motorbike to the palace gardens.
i Isabelle arrived at her Aunt Angelica's house.
j Porter met Jeanne in the garden.
k Angelica and Isabelle went clothes shopping.
l Teddy threatened Isabelle with a gun.

2 Listen and check.

3 Answer the questions below.

Why...

a is Detective Champion angry when he sees the white feather?
b is the 'Winged Victory' Porter's favourite statue?
c did Gabriel think the Angel must be a woman?
d did Angelica put a GPS tracker on the ruby necklace?
e did Angelica's puzzle need to be very difficult?
f did Angelica help Detective Champion find the jewellery?

4 Check your answers to Exercise 3 on page 16. Were you right? Why were the items important in the story? Discuss your answers with a friend.

5 **With a partner, role-play an interview with one of these characters.**

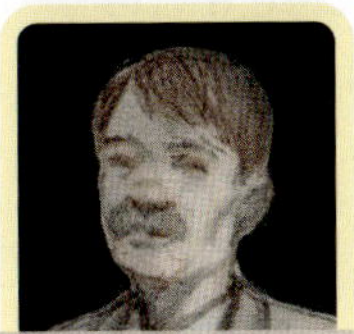
Detective Champion

Madame Helene

Sergeant Gabriel

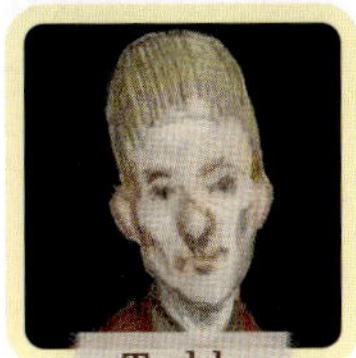
Teddy

Use the questions below.

- **a** What is your job?
- **b** What do you know about the Angel?
- **c** Do you want to catch the Angel? Why / Why not?

6 **Choose a different character, then think of some of your own questions to ask.**

7 **Read the extracts from the story, then answer the questions with a partner.**

Something happened many years ago – the first Angel saved his life, although Angelica never knew how. He made a promise at that time to protect the Angel and then to protect Angelica, too.

'Do you really need to find a new Angel?' […]
'I promised the first Angel,' she said. 'He was very special.'

'I can promise you, Detective, the room is perfectly safe. There is no way the Angel can take the crown out of this room!'

Her collection was complete. Ten years! Ten years and one hundred pieces of the most famous jewellery in the world. That was the promise she made to the first Angel, all those years ago.

- **a** Who makes a promise in each extract?
- **b** Who are they making a promise to?
- **c** Do they keep the promise in the story?
- **d** Is it important to always keep a promise? Why / Why not?

After Reading

Listen in and Speak

1 **Listen to the extract from the story. Then decide if the following statements are true. Discuss your ideas in pairs.**

a Porter cares about Isabelle.
b Porter was the first Angel.
c The first Angel was important to Angelica.
d Isabelle doesn't have any friends.
e Porter will miss Angelica if she leaves.
f Porter can drive.

2 **Listen to the extract. Discuss the questions in pairs.**

a How many characters are in the scene? Who are they?
b Have Sergeant Gabriel and Madame Helene spoken before? How do you know?
c Have Detective Champion and Madame Helene spoken before? How do you know?
d Where does Madame Helene work?
e Why isn't Detective Champion happy at the beginning of the extract?
f Why does Detective Champion apologise to Madame Helene about the necklace?

3 **Detective Champion wants to find out more about Madame Helene's job and interests. Write some questions for him to ask her. Work with a partner.**

4 **With a partner, choose some of your questions from Exercise 3. Role-play a conversation between Detective Champion and Madame Helene.**

5 Listen to the extract from the story. In pairs, decide which **TWO clues below relate to the extract.**

a

b

c

d

e

f

6 **Talk about each of the images from Exercise 5 in pairs.**

- What are they?
- What information does each clue give us about Gabriel?
- How do these things help Gabriel be a good police officer?
- How do these things help Gabriel be a good thief?

7 **Listen to the extract again. Discuss the questions in pairs.**

a What does Gabriel show Detective Champion on his laptop?
b Why doesn't Detective Champion like computers?
c What happened ten years ago?

After Reading

Listen in and Debate

GRAFFITI

1 What do these words mean? Discuss in pairs. Do you know other words associated with graffiti?

can
crew
spray
tag

Banksy is the most famous graffiti artist in the world. He started doing graffiti when he was 14. He hated school, and spray painting made him feel better about himself, and gave him a voice. Now he and his work are famous all over the world. However, no-one knows who Banksy really is. Much of Banksy's work has a political message. He speaks out against war, capitalism, and injustice, and takes sides with immigrants, the poor, and the homeless. Banksy did the graffiti above on a wall in Palestine. What is the message?

Is all graffiti art?

1 David

2 Solomiia

3 Marcos

4 Tamara

2 We asked this question to four teenagers. Who agrees? Listen and tick (✓).

3 Listen again and write the correct names.

a .... says graffiti can make a place seem unsafe.
b .... says that graffiti is an art form for young people.
c .... says that not all graffiti is good.
d .... says graffiti can bring artists together.

4 Think. Who do you agree with?

GRAFFITI AS VANDALISM

- aggressive
- ancient
- anti-social
- boring
- historical
- huge
- illegal
- private
- ugly

5 In pairs, read then complete with the adjectives in the box. Listen and check.

Not all graffiti is street art. Indeed a lot of it is a series of **(a)** ...., quickly (and often badly) written tags. These tags are at best **(b)** ...., and at worst **(c)** .... And there is an increase in **(d)** .... behaviour in areas with a lot of graffiti. Graffiti has destroyed **(e)** .... ruins, **(f)** .... buildings and **(g)** .... property. Governments all over the world spend **(h)** .... amounts of money cleaning and fixing damage done by graffiti. For this reason it is seen as a form of vandalism, and is **i** .... in many countries. However, many towns and cities have permission walls where street artists can paint without breaking the law.

DEBATE

6 In two groups, discuss the question below. Do you agree? Say why or why not. Give reasons and examples. Use the quotes to help.

Is all graffiti art?

I AGREE

BANKSY
(Graffiti artist and activist)

"Graffiti ultimately wins out over proper art because it becomes part of your city, it's a tool."

I DISAGREE

DAVID LYNCH
(Film director)

"Graffiti kills the possibility to go back in time and have the buildings be as they were."

After Reading

Cambridge English Exams

K A2 Key English Test Reading and Writing Part 4

1 Read the extract from the story.
Choose the correct word for each space.

Angelica was **1** .... on the sofa watching an old movie when the doorbell **2** .... She didn't get **3** .... It was 11 in the morning and she felt very lazy. There were no emails, so no replacement Angel. Angelica didn't know **4** .... to do.
Porter stood in the doorway of the living **5** ....
'Who is it, Porter?' asked Angelica.
'It is—' but before he could finish, **6** .... ran into the room.
'ANGELICA!' a voice shouted. Angelica jumped up.
'Isabelle!' It was her **7** .... They hugged and kissed **8** .... other on the cheeks. Angelica looked at her sister's daughter. She was taller than she remembered, and her hair was longer. But her eyes and smile were the same.

1 a lay	**b** lying	**c** laid
2 a played	**b** sang	**c** rang
3 a up	**b** down	**c** on
4 a which	**b** when	**c** what
5 a room	**b** place	**c** floor
6 a one	**b** anyone	**c** someone
7 a niece	**b** nephew	**c** daughter
8 a each	**b** one	**c** either

A2 Key English Test Listening Part 3

2 Listen to the extract from the story. Choose the correct answers.

1 Who has just arrived?
- a ☐ Angelica
- b ☐ Porter
- c ☐ Isabelle

2 Where is Isabelle's home?
- a ☐ Paris
- b ☐ Marseilles
- c ☐ Switzerland

3 Where does Isabelle study?
- a ☐ Paris
- b ☐ Marseilles
- c ☐ Switzerland

4 What is Isabelle's father doing in Paris?
- a ☐ working with the government
- b ☐ a gymnastics competition
- c ☐ Christmas shopping

5 What is Porter holding?
- a ☐ Angelica's schoolwork
- b ☐ Angelica's backpack
- c ☐ Isabelle's backpack

6 What does Isabelle ask Angelica?
- a ☐ If she can stay at her house.
- b ☐ What she is doing in Paris.
- c ☐ Where she can put her bag.

A2 Key English Test Reading and Writing Part 6

3 Write a text message (25-30 words) from Isabelle to Angelica. In the message:

- ask how she is;
- say what you are doing;
- ask if you can visit her.

After Reading

Exit Test

1 Listen and tick (✓) the correct picture.

a 1 ☐

2 ☐

b 1 ☐

2 ☐

c 1 ☐

2 ☐

d 1 ☐

2 ☐

2 K Read and complete with 1, 2 or 3.

a Louis XV's crown is complete with the famous Regent ....

1 jade 2 ruby 3 diamond

b The crown was displayed in a .... case.

1 ruby 2 glass 3 gold

c Angelica's email address was hidden on the .... of the statue.

1 moustache 2 hands 3 wings

d Angelica loves watching movies in the .... room.

1 dining 2 living 3 collection

e Porter picked up Angelica with a .... , after she stole the ruby necklace.

1 police car 2 motorbike 3 motorboat

f Gabriel wrote a computer .... to try to understand more about the Angel.

1 programme 2 virus 3 conference

g Angelica left a .... for Detective Champion so he could catch Terence.

1 message 2 puzzle 3 test

3 Look at the picture on page 26. Ask and answer questions about it.

Where are they?

What is Gabriel saying to Champion?

What are they looking at?

After Reading

Project

Missing masterpieces

In the story, Angelica steals Vincent van Gogh's *Poppy Flowers*. This is a real missing painting. It was stolen not once, but twice, from the same museum in Egypt. It is still missing today.

1 WEB Choose a painting from the list below and research it online.

- *Beach at Scheveningen in Stormy Weather* by Vincent van Gogh
- *Portrait of A Young Man* by Raphael
- *The Just Judges* by Jan Van Eyck
- *Portrait of a Lady* by Gustav Klimt
- *The Storm on the Sea of Galilee* by Rembrandt

2 Find the answers to these questions. Make notes.

- When was the painting stolen?
- Is it still missing? Or has it been found?
- Were the thieves caught? If not, are there any suspects?
- Where was the painting stolen from?
- Was it the only painting taken? Or was it stolen with other paintings?
- What other information is known about the theft?

3 Use your notes to write a short newspaper article about the theft.